This book belongs to: _____

A present from: _____

"Never forget you are an answer to prayer"

Three Little Lights

By Elizabeth Gan

ISBN: 978-0-9853642-4-3

Layout by David Ray of Ray Creative - www.raycreative.com

For my son, Jordan, and all the children of the world:

You are loved, you are wanted and you are an
answer to prayer. Always remember that.

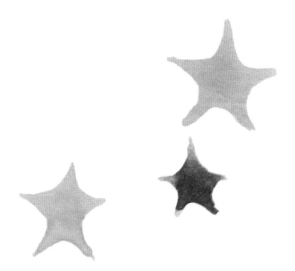

"A baby is God's opinion that the world should go on."

– Carl Sandburg

You are a dream wrapped up in skin, sent from heaven to earth, to be an answer to prayer.

You were no accident or surprise, but were planned for since the beginning of time. You are a melody released from the Father's heart that sings on earth.

The next time You look in the mirror, just remember that You look just like Him. You have His smile, His eyes and His laugh.

Always remember who You are...

Always remember You are wanted, planned for and loved...

Always remember that You are an answer to prayer...

From the edge of eternity's window, three friends stood peeking out at creation and the stars that hung far away.

It was their naming time—a time when all the little lights are called by the Father, named by him and then sent out to the earth to live for a while.

"What do you think it will be like down there? Do you think we will remember his face or the sound of his voice?" one little light said as they stared out at the stars.

"They say you forget, and I don't want to forget," he added.

"I don't know, but it looks so far away," said another.

"To be sent as a light carrier is an honor, but I don't want to forget him or his presence," said the last friend.

They turned to face him, as they could hear him walking towards them.

"Hello, I thought I heard voices out here. I have come to meet with you. It is your naming time.

The three looked at each other and smiled. "We were just looking out the window, and seeing how far it was," said one little light.

"I suppose it does look far away, doesn't it, from down there, but from where I stand, it's only a heartbeat away." said the Father, with a smile on his face.

"Are you ready, my little ones?" he continued as he held out his hand to them. The three took a few steps forward and stood on the palm of his hand.

One stepped forward.

Their eyes met as he leaned his head against hers and took a breath and began to sing over her...

"I call you 'Joy' because you will carry my smile everywhere you go. You are my Joy sent from my heart to the earth. You represent my heart and my laughter. When people see you, they will see me. You were sent for such a time as this, to bring my joy into people's lives. You are my song of joy on earth. I am so thankful for you. I love your smile, I love your giggle and your joy. And I love you. Take your song from my heart, and join in the symphony of life. Always remember your name and the one that named you. Always remember you are an answer to prayer.

You are my dream, wrapped up in skin and sent from my heart to the earth.

Always remember I love you."

She smiled back at him. His words rang in her heart and she felt a warmth of happiness flow through her.

Then he began to hum a tune over her. From deep within his belly his voice rumbled "mmmmmmmmmm."

As he did, his breath became light, and the song that he was singing got louder. It flowed between them back and forth as if he was teaching her how to sing her own song.

The music they created surrounded both of them, and the sight of her became lost in the cloud of gold swirls and glitter.

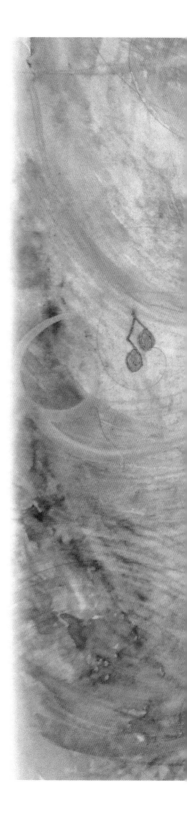

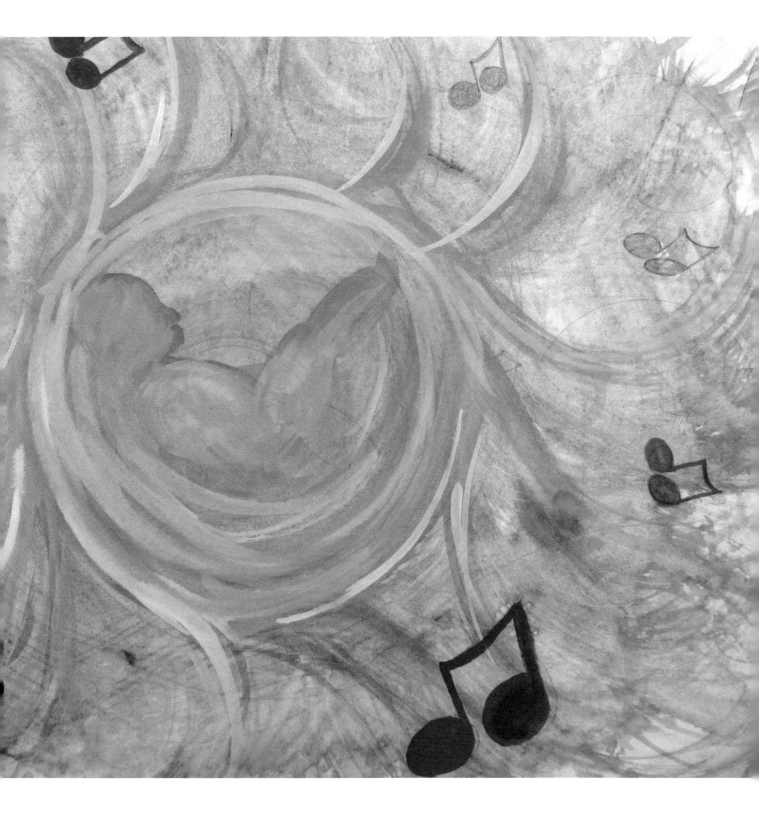

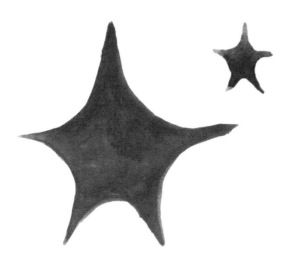

In a moment, her voice became louder, echoing off the walls of the great room where they were standing.

A bright light filled the room as Joy began to become part of the lights swirling above their heads.

She began to transform as both she and her song drifted out through the window.

In an instant she was flying out of the window and off towards the earth that waited outside, leaving the hall where they all stood, quiet.

Two lights
were left waiting
patiently on Father's hand.
He turned to face one of them and looking
deep into his eyes, took a breath and began to
speak:

"Your name shall be 'Samuel'. I am sending
you as a light bearer to the world because I have
heard the prayers of the people and am answering
by sending you. You shall be strong my son, and I am
already proud of who you are. You were sent to change
the world, to direct the others to me, and towards
home. You will know me when I call your name. You
will know it's my voice. I will never leave you, and my
words will always be upon your heart, my Spirit echoing
in your ears. Remember the sound of Love. Remember
that you are my son, and are an answer to prayer."
Samuel smiled and looked into the Father's eyes.
"Thank you," he said.

...ERS IN THE VALLE

YOU

HEART MY

YOUR LIFE

OUS
HEART IS NOT A ALL THE DAYS OF NEVER TAKE MY EYES OFF YOU

YOUR STRENGTH

MY CHILD, IN WHOM

The Father picked him up in his arms and held him close.

He began to hum a song over him, and the light of his breath flowed till all around them was a cloud of golden light and glitter.

Samyel started to sing along, and as he did, his form changed, and he started to float up into the heights of the ceiling. He began to sing his own song. With it echoing off the walls where they were, he flew towards the window and out into the space beyond.

In a moment, he was gone, and it was quiet again, leaving only one little light left.

"It is your turn, little one. Are you ready?" The Father said as he turned to face her.

Seeing the others transform and fly away from their home and the presence of the Father, she turned and said:

"Not really, Father."

"What is on your mind?" he said.

"I don't want to go because I don't want to forget your face, Father. I love you. I don't want to be parted from you."

The Father picked her up and held her close in his arms and said,

"It is true that you will not see me in the way you see me now, but I am there. I will never stop calling your name every day until you turn and listen. I promise we will meet again.

I promise to love you and be there for you, no matter where you are and no matter what you do. It's going to be OK. I love you all the way from heaven and back."

My eyes will never turn from watching over you. I will never stop pursuing you every moment of your life, and I will leave signposts for you to find that will point towards home.

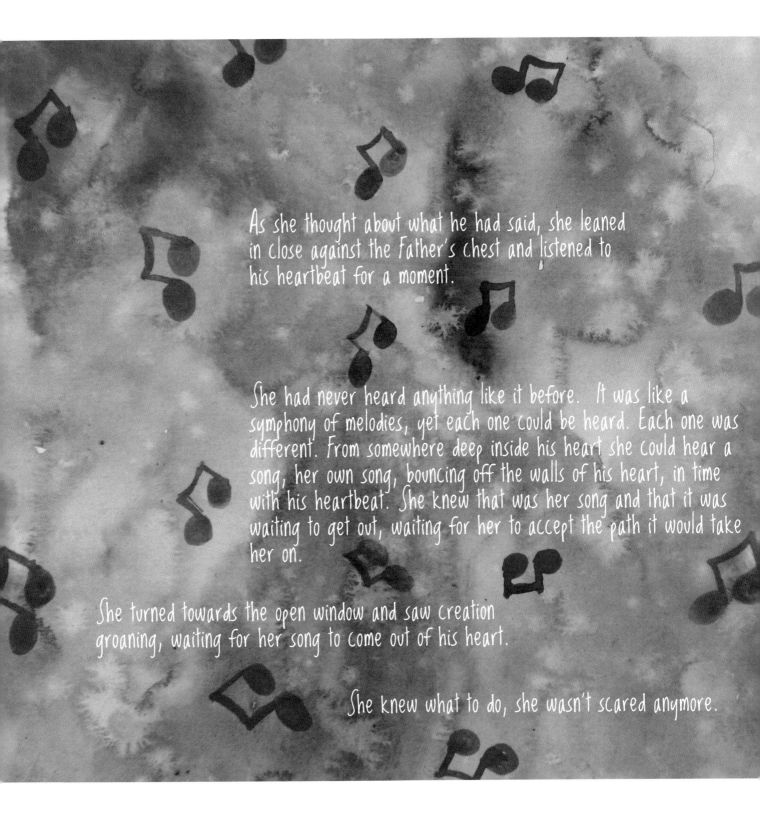

As she thought about what he had said, she leaned in close against the Father's chest and listened to his heartbeat for a moment.

She had never heard anything like it before. It was like a symphony of melodies, yet each one could be heard. Each one was different. From somewhere deep inside his heart she could hear a song, her own song, bouncing off the walls of his heart, in time with his heartbeat. She knew that was her song and that it was waiting to get out, waiting for her to accept the path it would take her on.

She turned towards the open window and saw creation groaning, waiting for her song to come out of his heart.

She knew what to do, she wasn't scared anymore.

She took a deep breath in and said, " OK, I'm ready now."

She climbed down off his lap and knelt before him. Their heads
touched and their eyes locked in a gaze.

He spoke, "I shall call you 'Anna', because you are full of my grace and
favor. Everywhere you go, the anointing of grace will surround you like
a trail of light because you carry my heart and you will carry my grace
also. Others will get to see my heart for them because you make it easy
for me to shine through you."

"You are precious to me, and I am
already proud of who you are."

"Always remember I love you, and never forget that you are an
answer to prayer. Go carry my light to the earth and shine as
bright as you can. I love you."

He took a deep breath in and breathed over her. He drew out the song that was buried deep in his heart named Anna and began to sing the melody into her being, until she was completely covered in light.

Floating up to the heights of the ceiling, she started to sing her own new melody that the Father had placed within her. In a moment, she headed for the window and then across the great divide, towards the earth.

"I'll see you soon, Anna, " he whispered as she flew out of the window.

The sounds of their songs were added to the symphony of creation as they flew towards the earth on the wings of light.

The Father watched as the little lights flew through the stars and towards earth.

"We will see each other again, I promise," he whispered after them with a smile on his face.

Three little twinkles of light sparkled from the earth as the lights landed. As if fireworks had gone off in his heart, he giggled to himself.

God never holds the circumstances of
your conception against you.

Nor does he hold the circumstances of
your birth against you.

He planned for you to be born exactly when
you were. You are not a mistake, and should
never accept that word over your life.

He never said that your life would be perfect, but he did
say he would be with you and he promised never to leave
you.

So turn your eyes and heart to heaven, and
remember the sound of his voice and your home.

He is waiting for you....

Psalm 127:3-5 Behold children are a heritage from the Lord. The fruit of the womb is His reward. Like arrows in the hand of a warrior, so are the children of one's youth. Happy is the man who has his quiver full of them. They shall not be ashamed.

Psalm 139v13 - 17 For you created my inmost being;
you knit me together in my mother's womb.
14 I praise you because I am fearfully and wonderfully made; your works are wonderful,
I know that full well.
15 My frame was not hidden from you
when I was made in the secret place,
when I was woven together in the depths of the earth.
16 Your eyes saw my unformed body;
all the days ordained for me were written in your book
before one of them came to be.
17 How precious to me are your thoughts, God!
How vast is the sum of them!

Jeremiah 1:5 Before I formed you in the womb I knew you, before you were born I set you apart; I appointed you as a prophet to the nations.

James 1:16 - 18 Don't be deceived, my dear brothers and sisters. 17 Every good and perfect gift is from above, coming down from the Father of the heavenly lights, who does not change like shifting shadows. 18 He chose to give us birth through the word of truth, that we might be a kind of first fruits of all he created.

Made in the USA
Charleston, SC
02 April 2014